I0623302

ENTREPRENEURSHIP - THE FUNDAMENTALS

A Handbook to Starting, Buying, or Operating a Business

NEIL HAMILTON

Copyright © Year 2024
All Rights Reserved by **Neil Hamilton.**

No part of this publication may be reproduced
in any form, or by any means, electronic or
mechanical, including photocopying, recording, or
any information browsing, storage, or retrieval
system, without permission in writing from Neil
Hamilton.

ISBN
Paperback: 978-1-965134-87-0

Dedication

To my wife Carol, with whom I have shared over 50 great years of marriage. To my children, Christine, Brian, and Michael, who make me proud every day, have enriched my life beyond words, and have blessed me with incredible grandchildren.

To those who dare to dream big dreams and make a difference in the world.

To North Central State College, which allowed me to share my experience and passion for small business with their students as an Adjunct Professor.

Acknowledgment

I believe that we were born into this world for a purpose, and while we may not realize that purpose when we are young, that purpose might become clear to us as we grow and mature. While we are on that journey to find our purpose, many people enter our lives, share that journey with us, and sometimes help us to find our purpose. These people share their love, friendship, experience, and wisdom with us without realizing how they have influenced our lives.

My mother shared her love with me in her own fashion and raised my two brothers and me mainly as a single mother, often not knowing how she would pay her bills. I didn't fully appreciate her plight and fears until I was older.

In January 2015, I was invited to join SCORE as a Certified Small Business Mentor. SCORE is a government-funded non-profit organization that mentors small businesses. It allowed me to share my experience and assist small businesses in achieving success.

Professor Lynn Jones invited me to speak to an Entrepreneurship class at North Central State College about business ownership. I was asked to stick around for a few minutes after the class. I was asked if I would have any interest in teaching that class. Imagine that. With no formal education beyond my high school graduation, I would be teaching Entrepreneurship and Small Business Management at a college. It piqued my interest. So, I joined the teaching staff at North Central State College as an Adjunct Professor and became the instructor for that Entrepreneurship class. What a great honor for me. Looking back after five years of teaching, I am unsure who learned more from the class, my students or me. It was a fantastic experience, and I am very grateful for the opportunity.

There are many managers I have worked under throughout my business career who will not be mentioned here. Some were good managers, and some not so much. In truth, I learned more from the bad managers than the good ones because I learned that people perform better when they are nurtured, supported, and shown that they are appreciated. These are traits that the bad managers did not exhibit.

WOB Accountants and Advisors of Ontario, Ohio - thanks for providing my book's Pro Forma, Income Statement, and Balance illustrations.

About the Author

Neil Hamilton is the President and CEO of Hamilton Insurance Group, Inc., in Mansfield, Ohio. He incorporated his business in 1992. He started from scratch as a one-man shop and has grown the agency into one of the largest and fastest-growing agencies in the region.

He was born and raised in Mansfield, Ohio, where he attended Mansfield City Schools and graduated in 1971. Neil learned early in life that working hard was the best way to get ahead. With no post-secondary education, he began his insurance career selling life insurance. Neil found that he had a talent for connecting with people, was a high-producing sales agent, and was among the top fifty producers company-wide at Western-Southern Life.

After nine years, Neil changed direction, took over a Nationwide Insurance agency, and embarked on his first journey into running a business. Realizing the constraints and limitations of representing only one company, Neil started his own business, which evolved into a company that owns and operates today.

Over the years, Neil has taken many business-related classes to further his education and knowledge of owning and operating a successful business.

In 2015, Neil was invited to join SCORE, a government non-profit charged with promoting and mentoring small businesses. This was a volunteer position, and Neil found that he had a passion for mentoring small businesses and helping them reach their goals.

In 2019, after speaking to an "Entrepreneurship and Small Business Management" class at North Central State College, Neil was asked to join the faculty as an Adjunct Professor to teach that same class. He taught at North Central State College for five years while still running his business. Neil still serves on the college's Business Advisory Committee. He has also served on several committees and boards for various organizations throughout the years.

Neil's Hamilton Insurance Group, Inc. is an award-winning business with two locations and twenty-two employees. It writes insurance for individuals and businesses in twenty-eight states. The agency represents over fifty insurance carriers.

Table of Contents

Preface

I was raised primarily by my divorced mother in Mansfield, Ohio. We were a lower-middle-class family with little expendable income. I learned early on that you need to work to earn money to buy something you want. So, at ten years old, I took over a paper route. This was actually my first venture into the business world. If you want to make more money, you increase the size of your route by adding more subscribers. My brothers and I all had paper routes. We learned valuable lessons early on. I am thankful for that upbringing.

At fourteen, I began working at a local grocery store. At sixteen, I got my driver's license, took a job where I could earn more pay, and continued there until I graduated from high school. I was a below-average student, and my prospects for success were not promising. I did not attend college and worked at the local General Motors Plant for three years after high school, where I was laid off three times due to labor cutbacks. I was asked to join Western-Southern Life as a life insurance salesman. I had no prior experience in sales of any kind, but I found that I had a talent for it. After passing the Insurance license test, I became the number two sales agent in the district in my first year and number one in year two.

In 1984, I changed direction and took over a part of a Nationwide Insurance Agency. I was an exclusive representative for Nationwide Insurance, meaning I only represented one company's products: Nationwide's. I was once again running a business, this time as an adult.

1992. I incorporated my agency and started my independent insurance agency. I am still the President and CEO of that corporation today and employ twenty-three insurance professionals.

I fumbled and stumbled until I began to find traction and grow. With no mentors to follow, I made many mistakes along the way. In time, I learned how to run a business, market it, and grow it. The company now has two locations with 23 employees in Ohio and is licensed in twenty-eight states.

I write this book to share my experience with others so they can learn from my mistakes. I also want others to know that success is still within their reach, regardless of their background, family's financial status, or limited education. The road to being a successful business owner is not easy, but it can be achievable.

This book is not a deep dive into all the nuances of owning a business. This book is simply a tool to provoke thought and arm you with the basic information that you need to make informed decisions when starting or running a business. It is not intended to replace the professional advice you should seek from an attorney or a CPA. On the contrary, I advise everyone to include these professionals as part of your team.

I wish you a successful journey into the business world. I am confident that this book will, in some small way, give you guidance and the confidence you need to succeed in entrepreneurship.

Chapter 1: The Reality of Entrepreneurship.

If you are reading this book, you are considering becoming an entrepreneur. The first thing you need to do is ask yourself, "Why?". Being an entrepreneur is not a job; it's a lifestyle. It's a commitment that will demand a great deal of your time and energy, not to mention the financial investment needed to get your business up and running.

The "Why" may be that you have a particular interest or passion driving you to choose this path. So, the next question is, can you turn that passion into a lucrative business that is sustainable and capable of providing income substantial enough to support you and perhaps a family?

When I started my business over thirty years ago, I had a passion for helping people and a desire to become my own boss. I had the ability to sell but no real experience in entrepreneurship. There was so much to know and so much to learn. Where and how was I going to gain the knowledge necessary for me to be successful? I was hesitant and fearful, as I had a family to support. That is why I wrote this book. I worked hard but I was not armed with experience, only passion. I am passionate about small businesses and want you to benefit from my experience.

When I began my journey, I had to weigh whether I was equipped with all the personality traits needed to pursue this course. These are some questions that I think you need to ask yourself.

Do I possess the knowledge needed in my chosen field?

Does my educational resume give me the knowledge necessary to be a business owner?

Do I have experience with the product or service I want to provide to my potential customers?

Do I have the financial resources needed to launch a business?

Many investors and financial institutions will be reluctant to invest in or loan money to a new business start-up.

I don't ask these difficult questions to discourage you but to provoke thoughtful planning and self-evaluation. This book was written to arm you with information that will help you make informed decisions before and after launching your business.

In performing a self-evaluation, let's explore the personality traits generally needed to be a successful entrepreneur.

- Education or experience in your chosen field
- A supportive family

- Time management skills
- Strong work ethic
- Organized
- Persistent
- Multitasking abilities
- Good health

Let's examine why these traits are important for starting a business. Being educated or experienced in your chosen field is essential. Imagine someone opening an auto repair shop but has never even changed the oil in his automobile. It's common sense. Right?

A business owner must invest much time and capital in their new venture, particularly someone who has just started their business from scratch. Their family must be supportive of that investment. They will spend much time away from their families and sometimes miss important family events, which can create great stress in the family dynamic. I was fortunate that my wife supported my decision, although it put a great deal of burden on her to try to keep things together at home.

There is a lot to do when trying to open a new business. There are also many distractions. Good time management skills will help you manage those distractions and finish your work. This also plays into being organized. Organizational skills will help you prioritize your workflow. It keeps you on task when many work-related chores demand your attention. When there is so much to do, a strong work ethic is a must to complete the tasks at hand. Sometimes, everything will seem to come all at once. Your ability to multitask will help you keep all the balls in the air.

The demands on your time and the financial commitment required to get your business up and running can create much stress, even for a healthy person. The stress of starting and running a business can magnify your health conditions.

If, after doing a self-evaluation, you feel confident that you have the personal traits to be successful, then you should explore the benefits of owning a business compared to the drawbacks.

The benefits might include:

- The pride you feel in building a business from scratch.
- The feeling of doing something important.
- The opportunity to profit from your creativity and efforts.
- The ability to make a difference in your community.

The drawbacks might include:

- A lower standard of living while you are building your business.

- Long hours and hard work.
- Uncertainty of income.
- High levels of stress.
- Potential failure and loss of investment.

Failure is always a possibility, even if you do everything right. The fear of failure will many times discourage someone from following their dream. Remember this: failure is not a life sentence. It's a life lesson. Actual failure is not trying. Don't give in to fear. Instead, let the possibility of failure encourage and motivate you to be resilient and keep pushing forward.

There are outside factors that could affect the success of your business. These factors may be beyond your control. These factors could be related to a change in your competitive position, high interest rates, or other economic factors. During the Covid epidemic, roughly 200,000 small businesses closed permanently, according to a WSJ article dated April 16, 2021. Many more companies have failed since then. A business failure can happen at any time. The following is an analysis of the U.S. Bureau of Labor performed from 2013 through 2023.

Time Frame	Percentage of Businesses That Fail
Within one year	23%

After 2 years	32.8%
After 3 years	36.2%
After 4 years	43.2%
After 5 years	48%
After 6 years	52.9%
After 7 years	56.6%
After 8 years	59.6%
After 9 years	62.2%
After 10 years	65.3%

The same report is broken down by industry.

Industry	Within One Year	Within Five Years
Food Service	14.20%	42.90%
Recreation	23.30%	43.50%
Construction	19.20%	43.70%
Educational Services	19.10%	43.30%

Finance and Insurance	22.60%	46.80%
Health Care	21.10%	42.20%
Manufacturing	17.60%	42.40%
Real Estate/Rental	17.80%	40.80%
Retail Trade	12.90%	40.20%

This is the reality facing many businesses. However, it doesn't have to be yours. Careful planning can help you avoid this outcome.

The more difficult the challenge, the greater the reward. You are not a statistic. You are on your own journey. As illustrated on the next page, your clients and the public might not know the challenges you will overcome on your journey. They will, however, see your success.

In the next chapter, we begin the journey, step by step, into exploring market research.

WHAT PEOPLE SEE

Accolades

Success

Awards

SUCCESS

Sacrifice   Disappointment

Persistence   Rejection

Focus

Determination   Sleepless Nights

                   Tears

Goals   Hard Work

WHAT PEOPLE DO NOT SEE

11

Chapter 2: Where do I Begin?

Entrepreneurship comes in all shapes and sizes. It can be diverse and vary by age, race, gender, and industry. There are home-based businesses, family businesses, and part-time entrepreneurs. You can start your business from scratch or buy an existing business. Each has its challenges and opportunities. We will begin with starting a business from scratch and discuss other business ownership options later in the book. Much of the research and many processes will be similar to other business ownership options.

Anyone can start a business, but not everyone can succeed. As previously discussed, you have to pass the self-evaluation test. *Do you have a marketable idea, product, or skill?* You may need a capital investment for a location, supplies, equipment, and marketing.

Where do you start?
What is your offering?
What is your value proposition?
What product or service are you offering that sets you apart from the competition?

These are all important questions that can be answered by performing a Feasibility Study. This process is a tool to help you examine various aspects of starting a business, such as who your customer base will be, a description of your product or service, your value proposition, what are the differentiators in your product offering, and do you have the qualified staff to develop your product and help you launch your business.

Step One:

It would be best to begin by researching your industry to evaluate its current status.

- Is your chosen industry growing?
- Is the industry generally profitable?
- What is the life cycle of the industry? Is it a product or service that will be needed far into the future, or will it become outdated due to changing technology and trends?

Much of your research can be done online or at your local library. You can gather information by first determining your industry's NAICS class code (North American Industry Classification System) from www.census.gov. You can also research trade associations by looking up the National Trade and Professional Association Directory at your local library. Using Google to research your industry is another efficient way of gathering information.

Another option in doing research is to look in your backyard. Are there other businesses in your local area offering similar products or services? Do they appear to be profitable? How will you differentiate yourself from them?

<u>Step Two:</u>

Let's examine who your customer base is.

- Is it a growing market?
- What are the demographics in the area where you will be doing business?
- Do the demographics show enough market size to support your business and your competition?

This information can be easily found by going to https://www.census.gov/quickfacts. You can type in the city or county where your business will be located. You can learn a lot about your community and the potential market for your product or service. Here is some of the information that is available on the website.

- Population trends
- Age of population by percentage
- Housing trends
- Median Income
- Total number of those employed

Once you have gathered this information, you can ascertain whether your community is growing and vibrant or shrinking and aging. For example, if you are building high-end kitchen cabinetry, does the housing trend indicate that new homes are being built that may create a market for your products? Does the median income indicate that the average income is such that consumers will be willing and able to pay for high-end cabinetry?

The answers to these questions will help you decide whether to proceed to the next step in your business evaluation process or not.

Step Three:

Next, you should examine your product or service and how it differs from similar products or services from potential competitors.

- What is your value proposition? Why would someone buy your product or service?
- What are the features and benefits that you are offering?
- Is your product less expensive to consumers?
- Do you offer a longer extended warranty?
- Do you offer better service or a better-quality product? Is it measurable?
- Does your product reach an underserved niche market?

When marketing your product or service, you must have a selling point that will distinguish your business from similar businesses.

Step Four:

- Does the launching of your business require a supporting cast?
- Do you need additional employees to help you develop and manufacture your product?
- Do you need trained staff to provide service to your future customers?
- Where will you find people to meet your needs?
- Will these people have the knowledge and skills to fill these roles in your company?

Step Five: Pricing

Your next step should be to determine your business cost and the amount of product you will need to sell to make a profit.

- What is the cost of the materials needed to manufacture your product?
- If you are a retail store, what will be the cost of purchasing the inventory to stock your shelves?
- If you are a service company, how many vehicles will you need to service clients?
- What tools will need to be purchased to provide the service?
- Do you need to stock an inventory of parts, and how much will those parts cost?

Research into the cost of inventory and parts, vehicles (if needed), insurance, labor, rent, utilities, computers, and technology is essential.

In performing this task, you can then ascertain how much income will be needed to turn a profit. How much product do you have to sell or service do you need to provide to make this venture worthwhile? It is best to carefully review these five steps before moving forward.

Step Six: What's in a Name?

Creating a name for your company is more important than you might think. The importance may vary according to the type of industry you are in. If you are a CPA or a legal firm, your name should exude confidence from your potential clients. If you are a retailer, you want to grab attention. You want to choose a name that people will remember. Be creative. Survey friends for ideas. Make it a fun exercise.

When I was mentoring a small business, the client asked me if the name they wanted to use for their company sounded "Cheesy." She was a little upset when I said "yes." Then I explained that it was a good thing. It applied to her art business and was memorable.

That is the point. Once you have settled on a name, go to your state's Secretary of State website and perform a name search to ensure that the name has not been registered by someone else.

Company Logo

Another fun exercise where you can involve others is creating a logo. Again, be creative. It should be easily recognizable. You can purchase software programs or have a professional advertising company create one for you. Brainstorming with friends, partners, and employees can help improve the creative process.

Once you have created your logo, you will want it to become your intellectual property. In Chapter 3, we will explore how to protect intellectual property.

Chapter 3: Intellectual Property

Patents

If you have created a unique product, you will want to protect it from unauthorized use or copying by a competitor. You can best achieve this by applying for a patent with the U.S. Patent and Trademark Office. A patent is only issued to an inventor who has created a unique product or design. Upon approval of your patent, your product or design will be protected from duplication or unauthorized use. This protection is usually for a period of twenty years.

These patents have been issued since 1790. Over 300,000 patents are issued yearly on products ranging from lightbulbs to peanut butter.

The application process requires a full explanation and description of the product you created, including a clear and complete diagram. Acquiring a patent can be grueling and can take two to three years for approval. A patent attorney can help you complete your filing and will continue monitoring the application's progress. This could cost you from two to five thousand dollars.

Trademarks

You will want to file a trademark application if you have a distinctive tagline, logo, design, or name.

You can search the government patent website to see if another business has filed that design. You may be disappointed if you want to include a name, logo, or design containing a surname. My attempt to protect my logo failed as my business contained my last name. While my design was unique, my name wasn't.

Even trying to protect a tagline can be difficult. I was threatened with a lawsuit because I had used a tagline for twenty years that I thought was too generic to register. Someone else did, and I was forced to discontinue.

Copyrights

If you are writing or publishing any written any type of creative written material such a book, signs, or even music you will want to contact the U.S. Copyright Office and apply for a copyright to protect your intellectual property. This will protect your work for a limited period of time. You can access information about copyrights by visiting https://www.copyright.gov

Chapter 4: Choosing Your Business Entity

This chapter will discuss various types of business entities and why choosing the right option is vital to your business planning process. There are five different types of business entities. Each type has advantages and disadvantages.

Sole Proprietorship:

If you are a small one-man operation, you might feel that a Sole Proprietorship will suit your needs. On the plus side, you only have to file taxes once. You alone are in charge of the business. Sounds like a good plan, doesn't it? However, you are solely liable for any claims made against the company. If you cause injury or property damage to another party while operating your business, you alone have the liability exposure. Generally, it's not recommended, as all of your business and personal assets may be at risk. Getting financial assistance through bank loans is more difficult to get as well.

Partnership:

Partnerships are often formed when two or more people create a business. Like a sole proprietorship, the liability for any claims will fall on all partners who share ownership in the business. On the other hand, like the Sole

Proprietorship, the income from the company will be reported on the partners' personal income tax. The Partnership does not pay taxes.

C-Corporation:

Filing your business as a C-Corporation has many advantages over a Sole Proprietorship or Partnerships. First and foremost, if your corporation is named in a lawsuit, you will not be personally liable; therefore, your personal assets will not likely be at risk. On the other hand, corporations are strictly regulated and are taxed twice. The corporation pays taxes, and the shareholders are taxed on dividend distributions.

'S' Corporation:

An 'S' Corporation, also known as a Subchapter Corporation, provides the same protections from liability claims as a C Corporation, but all corporate profit is taxed to the individual shareholders as ordinary income. The 'S' Corporation does not pay income tax. It is regulated similarly to the C Corporation. The ability to raise capital by selling stock shares is much more difficult.

Limited Liability Company (LLC):

The LLC is similar to the 'S' Corporation in that it protects the owners against liability exposures, and the profits are taxed as ordinary income to the LLC owners. S-Corps and LLCs are considered pass-through entities.

I have found that creating a legal entity such as a corporation or LLC is usually preferable as it will provide some protection for your personal assets.

It is important that you fully understand the benefits and risks of each of these options. I strongly recommend that you meet with your attorney and CPA before deciding.

Now that you have chosen which type of entity best suits your business needs, you should consider what name you will give your new company. The next step should be to do a business search on your state's Secretary of State's website. You may be unable to file for that name as another company may already use it. The name you file under the Secretary of State's office does not necessarily need to be the same name you operate under. You can choose a DBA (doing business as) name that differs from the corporate name; for example, your chosen corporate name may be The Smith Company, LLC, but you might use ABC Appliance Store as your DBA.

Once you have completed your name search, you can file your business entity with your Secretary of State. While you can do this yourself, I strongly recommend allowing your attorney to complete this process. Depending on your location and the legal firm you choose, you can expect to pay about $500 to $1,500 to get your business filed.

Once you have determined which entity best suits your needs, it is important to discuss how to create your business plan. As for me, my preference was the S-Corp option. This option allowed me to easily access company funds while protecting my personal assets from potential creditors.

Chapter 5: The Business Plan

A business plan is one of the foundations of your business. An appropriately crafted business plan tells your story. It describes who you are, what products and services you will provide, what your company's mission and vision are, and demonstrates what research has been done to show that there is a market for your product or service. I consider it as the road map to success.

You might ask, "Why do I need a business plan?"

A new venture will often find it challenging to attract investors. As we discussed earlier, many companies fail in their early years. The fact is, they don't plan to fail; they often fail to plan. While crafting a business plan isn't a guarantee that you will be successful, it does demonstrate that a great deal of thought, research, and planning was done before you began this journey.

There are several elements to a well-constructed business plan.

Title Page:

The title page should show the company name, logo, address, and contact information.

Table of Contents:

This should be self-explanatory. It should

illustrate the content and page number of each business plan section.

Executive Summary:

This section should summarize the operations and plans for the company.

- Who are the owners, and what are their experience and qualifications?
- What products and services will the business be offering?
- How will those products and services benefit consumers?
- Who is the target market? How big is the market for the products and services?
- What differentiators separate the business from other companies offering similar products and services?

This section should be short and to the point. It should not be more than one page. Think of it as an elevator presentation. How much can you tell someone about your idea while riding on an elevator with them?

Mission and Vision Statement:

Many prospective entrepreneurs often overlook this. Your mission statement explains the guiding principles that you want your company to exhibit. Who do you want to be, and what are your goals?

It speaks to your passion and commitment to excellence.

Your vision statement explains how you plan to achieve those goals. What is your action plan to achieve excellence? If you have no mission or vision for your company, how will you know when you have achieved success?

Here are a few examples of mission statements used by major corporations.

- Sony: To be the company that inspires and fulfills your curiosity.
- Facebook: To give people the power to share and make the world more open and connected.
- Google: To organize the world's information and make it universally accessible and useful.
- Microsoft: To enable people and businesses throughout the world to realize their full potential.

Your mission statement does not need to be long. It should speak to what your company is to achieve. Do you believe the mission statements above accurately describe what those company's images represent?

Products and Services:

In this section, you will describe in more detail what you will be offering in terms of products and services. If it is a product, how will you produce your product? Can you produce enough products to keep up with demand? What is its shelf life? How much does it cost to manufacture each unit? What will the profit per unit be? How many units must be sold to show a profit?

If you are providing a service, what will that service be? Who is your target market? Is the market for your services large enough to create an opportunity for sustainable revenue in the future? Do you have the training and experience to provide this service? How will your employees be trained, and how many do you anticipate hiring?

Before launching your business, these essential questions must be answered.

Competitor Analysis:

Who is your competition? What is your differentiator? Why will the consumer choose your product or service over your competition? Here, you will answer these difficult questions.

Potential lenders or investors need to understand how your business will outperform companies providing similar products or services. Perhaps you will have lower overhead and labor costs, allowing you to offer a lower price in the market. Maybe the quality of your product is better. Will you provide a better warranty on your product or service?

This is where you provide information about

the features and benefits of the product and services you will provide.

Marketing Plan:

There are many ways to market a product or service today, but being honest and genuine about the product is important. What will be your approach? There are more traditional ways, such as billboards, direct mail, newspaper-magazine advertisements, television, and radio. Many people today prefer to use social media. Social media has many options and is considerably less expensive than traditional advertising methods.

How you market your product or service may depend mainly on what that product or service is and who your target customer base is. If you are trying to reach an older audience, you will want to use a more traditional approach. A younger audience can be more easily reached through social media.

In this section, you will explain your approach and why.

Financials:

Finally, you will create your pro forma. A pro forma is a financial projection statement based on all of the market research you have done. You will estimate your revenue over the next twelve months and beyond. You will show how you arrived at those estimates. You will also show your anticipated cost of doing business. You should include location expenses such as rent, utilities, maintenance, etc. What will be the cost of materials, labor, employee benefits, advertising, and any other relevant expenses? What capital expenditures will be needed for equipment and supplies? How much cash do you have, and what are your total assets?

You may want to include your CPA when compiling this information. I believe that having a CPA involved in creating your financial statements will lend credibility to the numbers contained in them.

Pro Forma

The next page illustrates a Pro Forma created for a small manufacturing company. I believe the Pro Forma is an essential part of your business plan, as it should provide a realistic projection of your company's performance for the next four years. A well-thought-out Pro Forma might help lenders and investors gauge your readiness for your business idea.

I have found that dressing up your plan with graphics related to your business or industry provides a more finished and professional look to your proposal.

small manufacturer

Cash	25,000.00	5,000.00	72,537.00	96,912.56	125,707.55
Accounts receivable		82,191.78	41,095.00	41,095.00	43,149.80
Inventory and supplies	25,000.00	25,750.00	25,750.00	25750	26,750.00
machinery and equipment	450,000.00	450,000.00	450,000.00	450,000.00	450,000.00
accumulated depreciation	-	(64,300.00)	(128,600.00)	(192,900.00)	(257,200.00)
net property and equipment	450,000.00	385,700.00	321,400.00	257,100.00	192,800.00
Total Assets	500,000.00	498,641.78	460,782.00	420,857.56	388,407.35
Accounts payable		26,082.00	39,122.00	39122	41,187.07
Loc Pk400.00		11,264.77		-	
ltd 450000.00	450,000.00	384,826.13	337,084.58	276,181.16	212,214.42
equity beginning of year	50,000.00	50,000.00	66,369.50	84,627.07	105,556.03
nett income		16,369.50	18,257.57	20,928.96	29,451.48
Total liabilities and equity	500,000.00	498,642.40	460,783.65	420,859.71	388,409.00
sales		500,000.00	500,000.00	500,000.00	525000
cost of goods sold					
materials		200,000.00	200,000.00	200,000.00	216750
labor and benefits		75,000.00	75,000.00	75,000.00	75000
depreciation		60,000.00	60,000.00	60,000.00	60000
		335,000.00	335,000.00	335,000.00	351750
Gross Margin		165,000.00	165,000.00	165,000.00	173,250.00
general and admin		117,325.00	117,325.00	117,325.00	117325
depreciation expense		4,300.00	4,300.00	4,300.00	4300
interest expense term loan		21,249.00	18,421.57	15489.72	12,356.36
interest expense line of credit		300.00	600.00	0	
other expenses		143,174.00	140,646.57	137,094.72	133,981.36
income before tax		21,826.00	24,383.43	27,905.28	39,268.64
provision for income tax 25%		5,456.50	6,085.86	6,978.32	9,817.16
net income		16,369.50	18,257.57	20,928.96	29,451.48
cash flow					
net income		16,369.50	18,257.57	20,928.96	29,451.48
add depreciation		64,300.00	64,300.00	64300	64300
deduct principle reduction term loan		(55,074.00)	(57,891.55)	60853.4	(63,966.76)
deduct principal payment line of credit		(11,264.77)		0	
increase in accts rec 60 days		(82,191.78)	41,095.00	0	(2,054.80)
increase in inventory 5% sales increase		(750.00)	-	0	(1,000.00)
increase in accounts payable		26,082.51	13,040.75	0	2,065.07
increase (decrease) in cash		(31,264.77)	67,537.00	24,375.56	28,794.99
accounts receivable		60	30		30
sales		500000	500000		525000
accounts receivable		82191.8	41095.9		43150.68493
			41095.9		-2054.8
		90	45		45
accounts payable		317,325.00	317,325.00		334,075.00
		39081.51	39122.26		41187.32877
			19040.6		2065.07

Chapter 6: Financing Your Business

Knowing your funding options is imperative when starting, buying, or expanding your business. If you are starting a new venture in the U.S., you have the challenge of proving you are creditworthy. Can a financial institution take the risk? Upon reviewing your credit application, the potential lender will ask for the six 'Cs': character, capacity, capital, collateral, conditions, and cash flow.

They will immediately want to verify your trustworthiness. Do you have the *character*, business experience, and credit history to operate your business and repay the loan successfully? The lender will likely ask for financial references.

Capacity refers to how quickly you can get the business to profitability so that you can meet and exceed your expenses, including your loan payments.

How much personal *capital* have you invested in the business? Do you have a history of saving and being frugal in your spending habits?

What *collateral* do you have, such as tangible assets, property, equipment, and accounts receivables? Do you have any third-party guarantees?

What *conditions* are you seeking regarding the

loan length and amount? How will the funds be used?

Finally, where will the *cash flow* come from to meet the loan payments?

There are many options available when seeking funding for your business. In my opinion, the go-to has to be your local bank, where you have your personal accounts. Not all banks are good at commercial lending. Your bank may recommend an SBA loan if your business is a new venture.

An SBA (U.S. Small Business Administration) loan is guaranteed by the SBA, which alleviates the risk of the bank lending the money. Many banks will require this. The downside of an SBA loan is that it generally will take a little longer to get processed, there will be more paperwork, there will be interest involved, and the fees associated with loan processing may be higher.

There is an illustration of the first page of an SBA loan application on the next page.

SBA Loan

U. S. Small Business Administration
APPLICATION FOR BUSINESS LOAN

Individual	Full Address				
Name of Applicant Business					Tax I.D. No. or SSN
Full Street Address of Business					Tel. No. (inc. Area Code)
City	County	State	Zip		Number of Employees (Including subsidiaries and affiliates)
Type of Business			Date Business Established		At Time of Application ____ If Loan is Approved ____
Bank of Business Account and Address					Subsidiaries or Affiliates (Separate for above) ____

Use of Proceeds: (Enter Gross Dollar Amounts Rounded to the Nearest Hundreds)	Loan Requested			Loan Request
Land Acquisition		Pay off SBA Loan		
New Construction/ Expansion Repair		Pay off Bank Loan (Non SBA Associated)*		
Acquisition and/or Repair of Machinery and Equipment		Other Debt Payment (Non SBA Associated)		
Inventory Purchase		All Other		
Working Capital (Including Accounts Payable)		Total Loan Requested		
Acquisition of Existing Business		Term of Loan - (Requested Mat.:		Yrs.

CURRENT AND PREVIOUS SBA AND OTHER GOVERNMENT DEBT: Complete the chart for the following: 1) SBA loan applications pending for the applicant or any of its affiliates; 2) Federal debt, including SBA, received by the applicant including loans that have been paid in full or charged off; 3) Federal debt (including student loans and disaster loans) borrowed by any principal of the applicant; 4) Federal debt borrowed by any other business currently or previously owned by any principal of the applicant. If there has been a loss to the government as a result of a charge off, compromise, or discharge due to bankruptcy for any of the listed debt, it must be identified below. LOSS is the outstanding principal balance of the loan that the government agency had to write off after all collection activities (including compromises) were finalized.

Name of Agency	Borrower's Name	Original Amount of Loan	Date of Application	Loan Status	Outstanding Balance	$ Amount of Loss to the Gov't
Agency Loan #						
#		$			$	$
#		$			$	$

ASSISTANCE List below the name(s), occupation, and address of anyone (including the lender) who assisted in the preparation of this form and who received or will receive compensation from the applicant for this assistance. For any person listed, an SBA Form 159 must be completed by the applicant and listed person and submitted as part of the application. The lender must complete the "Lender's Certification" on any SBA Form 159 prior to the loan being approved.

Name and Occupation	Address	Total Fees Paid	Fees Due
Name and Occupation	Address	Total Fees Paid	Fees Due

Note: The estimated burden completing this form is 12.0 hours per response. You will not be required to respond to collection of information unless it displays a currently valid OMB approved number. Comments on the burden should be sent to the U.S. Small Business Administration, Chief, AIB. 409 3rd St., S.W., Washington, D.C. 20416 and Desk Office for Small Business Administration, Office of Management and Budget, New Executive Building, room 10202 Washington, D.C. 20503 OMB Approval (3245-0016) PLEASE DO NOT SEND FORMS TO OMB. SUBMIT COMPLETED APPLICATION TO LENDER OF CHOICE.

SBA Form 4 (2-05) Previous Edition Obsolete   Page 1

There are other financial organizations available

as well that may provide commercial lending. You may consider different ways of raising money for your business. You could seek a small business grant, or you can use crowdfunding.

There are different types of crowdfunding.

- Reward-Based - You are developing a new product. Once it has been manufactured, you can give each investor a free product.
- Equity-Based – This option appeals to venture capitalists who are seeking a return on their investment. These funders are shareholders in the business.
- Donation-Based – This approach is similar to Go-Fund-Me. The upside to this approach is that it is a donation and does not need to be paid back. The downside is that you are not likely to get much traction with this, as the donations will likely be small.
- Debt-Based – Investors will fund your request with the anticipation of getting repaid with interest.

The crowdfunding approach requires a robust online marketing campaign using various social media platforms, and several platforms are available.

Chapter 7: Launching Your Business

You have completed your self-evaluation, completed your market research, crafted an honest and detailed business plan, filed your business entity, secured funding for your business, and are ready to launch.

Not quite yet.

Several factors can impact the success of your business. You should consider whether your location suits your target client base. Is your pricing in line with your competitors? What is your plan for the distribution of your products and services? Do you have a marketing strategy to reach your targeted client base? Have you created a website for your business? Have you created a social media presence on the most popular platforms? We will discuss these issues in this chapter.

Location:

For many industries, such as retail, food service, wholesalers, or service companies, choosing the right location can be critical to your success. It would be best to consider who your client base is and where that base's highest concentration is. Once you have determined that, you can search that area.

For example, if you are a restaurant or a retail

store, then you may want to be located in a high-traffic area where you would have high visibility. Restaurants tend to cluster. Where there is one, you will likely see more. The same is valid with retailers. Retail stores do very well in malls and shopping plazas. They feed off each other's traffic. Stand-alone retailers don't tend to perform as well; they can only rely on the traffic they can attract to their location.

Location may not be your top priority for a service-oriented company, such as a graphic designer, home improvement contractor, or janitorial service company. You will want to ensure that the space you are buying or leasing is large enough for your current and future needs. I was once told to take the square feet I need now and add another 50 percent when considering a location for my business. This will allow for future growth.

Distribution:

When selling a product, determining your chosen distribution model is your top priority. Traditionally, a retail store location has been used to sell products. Today, there are many more options available. A physical location is still popular as many consumers like to see and touch the products they buy. However, there is more overhead associated with a storefront. You will have building maintenance, staffing, utilities, rent, etc.

Selling directly to consumers using the internet is another option. Currently, 63% of shopping journeys begin online. You can use various platforms such as Facebook Marketplace, eBay, Shopify, or Amazon. The fees associated with using these types of platforms will vary by platform. Shopify will charge anywhere from $39.99 to $399.00 per month. eBay charges $7.95 monthly or $4.95 monthly on an annual plan. The dominant player in online sales is Amazon. You can create an Amazon account as an individual and sell your products for as little as $ .99 per sale or register under their Professional Plan and pay a $38.99 monthly fee. These prices are as of May of 2024.

The advantage of using an existing platform is that these sites have a strong internet presence and millions of daily users. If you were to create your own website, you would have to spend thousands of dollars to develop it and thousands more for search engine optimization (SEO).

It doesn't have to be an either-or situation. You can sell products from a physical location and sell them online as well using multiple online platforms.

Pricing Strategies:

Pricing strategy options may differ by industry.

The one thing in common is everyone wants to make a profit. The common denominator is the formula for determining the cost of doing, including the location expenses, labor, materials/inventory, and advertising.

When you determine the cost of doing business, you will look at the products and services you sell or provide and at what price you can sell them and remain competitive with your competitors. When you created your pro forma projections, you estimated how many products or services you would sell. You can then break it down per unit or service.

Businesses use several pricing strategies.

- Odd Pricing: Odd pricing is a simple strategy for making products appear less expensive to consumers. For example, instead of pricing an item at $10.00, a retailer may price it at $9.99.

- Freemium: A business may offer a base service or product for free but charge for upgrades and equipment to make the product's functionality more useful.

- Price Anchoring: Sometimes, you will see two or three very similar products in appearance and functionality sitting next to each other. The product difference is primarily price, i.e., a $500 watch setting next to a $1,000 watch in a display case. The mark-up on the products may be similar to the retailer. The $500 watch is a great deal.

- Price Lining: When a business offers a variety of products or services with a good, better, or best scenario, this is price lining.

- Subscription Pricing: When you sell a service where there is an ongoing fee to keep the service, this is subscription pricing. Subscription pricing can also be combined with a major purchase, such as a new furnace. The HVAC company may attempt to upsell the consumer by offering an annual service call to help maintain the furnace for an additional charge at the time of purchase.

- Loss Leader: Sometimes, a retailer will sell a product at or below cost to attract customers to their store, hoping that while the customer is in the store, they will also make additional purchases.

These strategies have been used for many years and have proven to be effective.

Launching Your Business:

Once again, you have done your self-evaluation, completed your market research, crafted an honest and detailed business plan, filed your business entity, and secured funding for your business.

In addition, you have chosen a suitable location and established your distribution and pricing strategies.

Another valuable step is to join your local chamber of commerce and any appropriate trade association that shares your business industry's purpose. These organizations will often assist you with promoting your new venture and perhaps hold a ribbon-cutting ceremony for your business.

I joined several community and professional organizations. I have found that there are many networking opportunities available through your local Chamber of Commerce. Service clubs have also allowed me to meet new people and network. Professional or trade associations also provide you with educational opportunities that help you grow in knowledge and understanding of your profession and markets.

It appears that you are ready to launch, but there is still one step left. You must file for a Federal Tax Identification Number (EIN). You can do this online by going to www.irs.gov.

You can start your business from scratch or choose other options, such as buying a franchise or acquiring an existing business. These options will be discussed in the next two chapters.

Chapter 8: Franchising

Thus far, we have discussed the processes involved in starting a business from scratch. Most of those processes will apply to any form of business ownership. A self-evaluation is still needed. You will need to do a pro forma and create a business plan. You may still need to seek funding.

In this chapter, we will discuss another way of becoming an entrepreneur. In my opinion, buying a franchise is a good option for many prospective entrepreneurs. This is particularly attractive in the food service industry, where franchise owners own most fast-food restaurants. There might be many benefits to following this path, and there are also different types of franchises.

Trade-Name Franchising:

This type of franchise involves purchasing the rights to use a brand name. An example is True Value Hardware. While the franchise owner will sell True Value-branded products, they are not limited to selling only True Value-brand products.

Product Franchising:

When you franchise to sell a specific brand or line of products, you are Product Franchising. This is typical when an auto dealership sells Ford or Toyota vehicles. Some dealerships represent multiple brands from the same property but usually require separate buildings for each auto manufacturer. Product franchising is also used in food service when they only offer Coke products or Lays Potato Chips.

Pure Franchising:

When franchising under Pure Franchising, you must meet very strict criteria regarding location, location layout, decor, Signage, and product line. McDonald's, for example, requires that you have over $500,000 in liquid assets and pay an initial franchise fee of $45,000. Additionally, you will spend eight percent of your annual gross sales. Part of this is a brand fee, which helps pay for national advertising. When you include the cost of real estate, a building, and equipment, you can expect to shell out between 1 $\frac{1}{2}$ to 2 $\frac{1}{2}$ million dollars to open the doors. This assumes you can purchase a franchise in the area you want to locate. Franchises tend to be very territorial. I think this is a benefit for most franchise owners. Much is the same with most other food service franchises.

If food service does not appeal to you, many other opportunities exist to purchase a franchise. For instance, restoration and cleaning companies may interest you.

What are the benefits of franchising? In general,

you will be part of a well-recognized national brand. You will normally receive thorough training from professionals experienced in your field. There is a proven business model to follow, and your location will be protected from an over-saturation of competitors selling the same brand products and services. These benefits give you a greater chance of building a successful business.

Financing a new business venture is always a challenge. Some franchise companies may be able to assist with securing financing. Also, I think that banks may be more open to funding a franchise purchase as they know that franchise companies will do extensive research before approving such a purchase.

Chapter 9: Acquiring an Existing Business

Is buying an existing business a good idea? That depends. I have completed several acquisitions over the years and found each one to be unique. Again, you must begin this journey with a self-evaluation. How familiar are you with the industry? Do you have the capital to make such a purchase, or can you secure the necessary financing? Will the current owner assist with the funding by carrying some of the debt?

Many questions need to be asked and answered. Why is the business available for purchase? Is the owner retiring, or are there other pressing concerns? Do you possess the experience in business management, knowledge, and talent to lead your new company to a successful future? This chapter will explore the benefits and pitfalls of acquiring an existing business.

Let's begin by exploring the company's historical data, such as the market that the business serves. Has the business demonstrated consistent growth in the last three to five years? Is this market a thriving market with room for future growth, or is it an industry that will soon become obsolete due to new technology? Is this company prepared to evolve and grow with changing times? These are essential questions. After all, you don't want to invest in a business whose product has a short shelf life and will soon be outdated. With this in mind, researching not only the business's financials and past growth but also the products and services produced by the company is necessary. If you are providing parts for a product that will soon be obsolete or selling a product with no room for future growth, then you are likely making a bad investment.

Today, there is so much data and information online that research information is easy to find. For example, Google searches for various market growth potentials are easy to find. The more research you do, the more likely you are to be successful in your acquisition journey.

Buying an existing business has advantages and disadvantages. Let's review the benefits and pitfalls of such a transaction.

Advantages

- The business is established and has a reputation in the marketplace.
- The existing business has an established customer base.
- The company has a location.

- The company has supplier relationships and inventory.
- The company has historical data, including financial information and past sales records.
- The company may have experienced and loyal employees.
- Financing for an existing business with a track record of success should be more accessible.

Assuming all this is true, this is a great starting place. A new business venture would have none of these benefits.

So, what could go wrong? Let's look at the disadvantages.

Disadvantages

- With the change in ownership, clientele could be lost because of the loyalty and goodwill established by the prior owner.
- Employees may look for positions with other employers, including competitors, and take with them vital information about your new company.
- There may be hidden debt or liability exposures not disclosed or known at the time of the purchase.
- Is the company's reputation still in good standing?
- The equipment and inventory may be outdated or in disrepair.

- Could the change in ownership affect the employees' attitude and loyalty?
- Does the existing business location optimize the business's success, or does it inhibit it?

The disadvantages are substantial, but most of these challenges can be overcome. Before the purchase, many steps can be taken to ensure a smooth and efficient transition from the current business owner to the new one. So, where do we start?

Steps For a Successful Process

Here is a list of steps you can take to avoid or minimize your exposure to unpleasant surprises.

- Do not buy the legal entity unless it is a publicly traded company. The current corporation, LLC, or other entity may have debt and/or liability exposures from prior events. Buy the name, the assets, and goodwill only. This is known as an asset purchase. In your purchase agreement, it should be explicitly clear that you do not accept any liability for prior acts of the business.

- Your agreement should include language requiring the prior owner to remain an employee for a predetermined period to assist with a smooth transition. This may help you retain your employees and suppliers until they are comfortable with the new ownership, and it could also help you retain existing clients.

- Examine all equipment and inventory to ensure everything is up-to-date and functional before your purchase.
- Request three to five years of financial information, including taxes, profit and loss reports, and balance sheets. Each report is only a snapshot in time, but by reviewing multiple years, you can see whether the company is showing a positive or negative trend. This can be a guess of what's to come.
- Request full disclosure of all debt carried by the company and liability exposures caused by past incidents.
- Sign a confidentiality statement restricting the current owner and the buyer from disclosing the nature of their negotiations. The release of information about a potential sale of the business can be harmful to all parties concerned. Employees may seek other employment due to job security concerns. Clients may look for other vendors, and suppliers could become uneasy.

So, the process of purchasing a business is a step-by-step process. Once you have determined that there is a business you want to purchase, you should begin to do a self-evaluation to determine if this is a business that you want to invest in. Is this the kind of work that you want to do? Do you have the knowledge, capital, and training to be successful? You would then research the industry to confirm that it is a growing industry that can be relevant for many years to come.

You must now contact the owner to express your interest in his business. Once you have confirmed the owner's desire to sell, you will both sign a non-disclosure statement. You would then sign a letter of intent. This shows that there is a serious interest in obtaining ownership of the business. That is when the hard work begins. You would be well advised to seek legal counsel to help you through this negotiation process and craft a sales agreement. This assumes that you followed the previous steps in researching the business, reviewing the financials, and so on. You would also want to have a CPA review those financials and create a proforma that will help guess the future financial feasibility of the company. You would also begin creating your business plan. The Proforma should be part of your business plan. In chapter four, we discussed the elements of a business plan.

In your research process, you should perform a SWOT analysis. This is a process of listing a company's strengths, weaknesses, opportunities, and threats. It may also reveal whether you yourself will be a strength or weakness for the company.

Facilities

In your research process, you will need to investigate the viability of the location. Is it suitable for future growth? Does the current business owner own the property as well? Will the property be part of the purchase? If the property is leased, what are the conditions of the lease agreement? How many years remain on the lease agreement, and will it transfer to a new owner? If there is a lease, is it a triple-net lease? That type of lease would not only include the utilities but may include maintenance, property taxes, etc. This is common, but you must be aware of what is included. Increases in property taxes, etc, will increase your expenses in the future.

What Is the Business Worth?

Determining the value of an existing business can be challenging, and there is no one-size-fits-all solution. The method used may vary by industry. Many factors are to be considered, including real estate, inventory, equipment, clients (book of business), and goodwill.

Real estate can be simple. Have the property appraised. What about the inventory? The age and relevance of the inventory or stock may somewhat skew the value. Has the inventory been sitting around for an extended period of time because it didn't sell? Does that inventory have a shelf life that may expire soon? Is the equipment used? What is the age of the equipment, and does it have a short life span where it will need to be upgraded, repaired, or replaced?

One of the most important assets may be the business's employees. Attracting quality, experienced staff can be challenging. If the business already has a solid staff, the next question may be, will they stay once the company is sold? While there is no accurate way to determine the value of these employees, it is an important consideration. Businesses have been purchased primarily to acquire the talented staff employed by the business.

The current client base (book of business) has intrinsic value. This is common in service organizations such as accounting firms, legal firms, doctor's practices, etc. Multiples of the annual revenue or profits often determine the value of these types of businesses. Another common way to evaluate a business is through an EBITDA calculation. EBITDA stands for Earnings Before Interest, Taxes, Depreciation, and Amortization. It is not uncommon for the buyer to pay several times the EBITDA calculation.

Again, having your own CPA involved in the valuation process is strongly recommended. There is a plethora of formulas that can be used to evaluate a business. Your CPA can provide guidance in determining which is best for your situation. Another option is to hire a professional valuation company that both you, as the buyer, and the current owner can agree on. Depending on the size of the business, this could cost several thousand dollars.

Determining the actual value of the business is tricky. The owner will always feel like it's worth more than a potential buyer, as they have poured their heart and soul into the company for many years. Emotions are involved, so everyone needs to be open and honest in the negotiating process. Having attorneys or another third party involved in the process may be the best solution.

An amicable transaction where all parties are satisfied with the final result is essential for a smooth transition.

Once you have determined the purchase price and secured the financing (if needed), you need to review the purchase agreement. The purchase agreement should list all of the assets to be included in the sale, including the company name, website, and phone numbers. A non-compete agreement is a very important element that needs to be included in the purchase agreement. The seller should not be able to sell you his business and turn around and start a new company that would compete with the business they just sold to you. They could steal your employees and your clients, causing you to lose a great deal of revenue and perhaps shut down your new business.

Transition Phase

You have done your due diligence, completed your research and business plan, completed the negotiations, transferred the business ownership into your name, and are now the proud business owner. Congrats! Now what?

A positive transition stage is crucial to a successful beginning of your entrepreneurship journey. There is much to do. Hopefully, you have secured the cooperation of the prior owner to assist with a seamless transition. You will immediately need to contact your suppliers, utility companies, and clients to reassure them that it's business as usual. You will need to gain control of the phone numbers, website, social media, and software passwords immediately.

What about your new employees? Do they feel safe and secure in their current jobs with a new owner in charge? Maybe not. If you want to retain them, you must address their concerns early on. So, what message do you want to convey? What kind of ownership-management style do you want to exhibit?

You want to get off to a good start. Food is often a good icebreaker. Bringing in breakfast or lunch for a staff meeting is usually an appreciated gesture. When you introduce yourself and speak to your employees, you want to reassure them that their jobs are not in jeopardy and that you intend to carry on many of the traditions, benefits, and pay levels that are currently in place. Convey a positive message of continuity as well as growth.

A self-evaluation and survey regarding the staff's level of knowledge, experience, need for training, and concerns is a great way to familiarize yourself with your employees. This will allow them an opportunity to be heard and show that you care about their thoughts and attitude toward the company. You can't fix it unless you know what is broken. You may also be able to sort out the glass-half-empty employees from those with a glass-half-full attitude. Depending on the number of employees involved, I have always found it valuable to meet with each employee individually to discuss their surveys and concerns. Again, the employee feels that you value their opinions while allowing you to learn a great deal about them and their needs. This could uncover valuable information that would not have been apparent during the purchase process.

Chapter 10: E-Commerce

The first recorded e-commerce sale was made for $12.48 on August 11, 1994. Since then, trillions of dollars in merchandise have been sold worldwide. This growing and expanding market is where almost anything can be sold online. In 2023 alone, it is estimated that over 1.1 trillion dollars of merchandise was sold online in the United States, nearly a 10% increase over 2022. Clearly, there is much opportunity to benefit from e-commerce.

Some may feel that this is not necessarily a good thing. With the growth of e-commerce, we have seen a substantial decline in the number of retail store locations. Macy's has closed 300 stores since 2015, and JCPenney has closed 175 since 2021. We are seeing many more empty retail stores nationwide as online sales increase. Since 2008, over 56,000 retail stores have closed, causing a loss of around 670,000 jobs.

That is the bad news. The good news is that there is a great deal of opportunity to grow a business without having a physical storefront. Your website becomes your storefront. According to Forbes, 62% of consumers shop more online now than they did pre-Covid. Physical storefronts are expensive. You have rent, utilities, equipment such as clothing racks and shelves, and the cost of employees.

With e-commerce, you have the wholesale price of goods, shipping costs, storage space, website maintenance, and Search Engine Optimization (SEO). Depending on the size of your online presence, you may not even have to hire employees.

Many retailers have been successful in selling online while maintaining physical locations. In fact, most major retailers are successfully selling goods using multiple methods.

So, where do you begin your e-commerce journey? What do you want to sell? Do you have a passion for creating art, jewelry, or other products that consumers are willing to buy, and you don't have to work full-time to run the business? You can continue your 8 to 5 job and sell goods online simultaneously. You don't have to work specific hours to have an online business. That gives you a great deal of flexibility.

To begin your journey in e-commerce, once you have identified what you want to sell, you will need to explore your options, and there are many.

There are four types of e-commerce.

- Business to consumer (retail goods)
- Business to business (services benefiting other businesses)

- Consumer to consumer (FB Marketplace)
- Consumer to business (SEO, influencer)

When starting an e-commerce business, your first consideration is what platform or website to use.

Website

Should you create your own website (which is not a good idea unless you are a professional web designer) or have a professional web designer build one? This option allows you to create one for your specific needs. The downside, of course, is that the cost may be thousands of dollars to develop. The more pages you have, the more robust the features and the greater the cost. You then have the cost of registering or buying a domain name and hosting fees. These costs are relatively low.

Your website should have an attractive aesthetic design. The images should illustrate the products and services you provide and sell. In other words, if you sell products that appeal to senior citizens, you should have images of the products or the services that attract them.

Your website should be easy to navigate. Sometimes, less is more. Too much clutter can confuse visitors. Make it easy for them to find what they are looking for. Hotlink buttons take website visitors directly to a specific product line, saving time for prospective customers. Product information and pricing should be easily visible. Informational videos can be incorporated into your site to educate consumers about specific products or services.

Chat:

You can further enhance your website by adding a chat feature. This lets customers chat with a salesperson or customer service representative in real time. For this to be effective, you need a dedicated person who can greet website visitors when they enter your page. Engaging with customers in real time can assist them with their purchasing decisions, increase sales, and improve customer satisfaction.

Traffic:

You then have to attract an audience. SEO optimization can help potential clients find you and your products. You will use keywords associated with your products or services on your website to help people find you. For example, in the real estate business, using terms like 'homes for sale' or 'property listings' on your website will help those searching for real estate options find your site. The SEO optimization will help your page align with the algorithms used in Google searches and help you show up near the top of the list for those seeking quotes or information online.

Social media can be a valuable tool in driving traffic to your website. You can advertise special offers, sales items, and new product or service offerings at little or no cost. You can build your audience through social media, which should, in turn, drive more traffic to your website. The key is to keep your audience engaged frequently by posting offers. We will discuss this more in Chapter 11.

Another great option is to use an e-commerce platform. There are many great options, and the cost is relatively low. You can choose a Shopify template design for as low as $29.00 monthly. Other options include WIX, Square Online, Web.com, and Big Commerce, to name a few. Each platform has hundreds of templates and varied pricing strategies. Some may charge transaction fees and fees if you want to change templates. Another benefit of using these platforms is that security protocols are in place to protect businesses and consumers.

Other options for selling goods online are Amazon.com, Walmart Marketplace, and eBay. Using Amazon as a small business would cost about .99 cents per transaction. To set up a professional account, you would pay a monthly fee of $39.99.

Your success is only limited by your creativity.

Chapter 11: Crafting a Marketing Strategy

Before crafting a marketing plan, you need to identify your target market client and ascertain who your primary competition will be. Different industries will obviously have different strategies regarding how and where they spend their marketing dollars. Once you have identified the demographic you want to target, you need to establish the potential client's characteristics. You can then begin to determine the needs of that client base. When you implement your marketing plan, you can focus your marketing on those needs.

Now that you know what demographic you want to reach, you will want to do market research to determine the size of that demographic in your target area. If you are a storefront type of business, you will want to search within your geographical location. What is the size of that market within driving distance? This research is called data mining. This information is available on the Internet or at your local library.

Once you have established your target market and the size of that market and have determined what the needs are for that market, you should analyze your company's advantages versus your competition. If your competition is a big box store, they can sell cheaper due to their high sales volume. Higher volume means that they can negotiate with suppliers to purchase merchandise at lower prices than a small business can. So, what is your value proposition? How do you differentiate yourself from your competition? You need to be creative. You need to be unique. You need to find your niche. A big box store may seem impersonal and not connected to the community, whereas a small business can easily network within the community through community involvement.

While many people price-shop and shop wherever they find the cheapest price, others look for value, quality, and a connection with the business. This is where the small business can excel. When shopping at a big box store, you may have trouble finding someone to wait on you and help you find an item you are looking for, and when you do find someone, they may tell you it's in aisle 25. A small business employee will more likely walk with you to the aisle and show you the various options that are available. You may pay a little more, but a different buying experience brings the customer value. That is a differentiator.

There are many ways a small business can carve out a loyal client base in a community. Get involved. Join your local Chamber of Commerce and attend chamber events. Sponsoring events is better yet. Create a professional image with other businesses so they see you as an expert in your field. Brand your business as the business of choice for your industry. Perception becomes a reality for many people. Much of this can be accomplished on the cheap by using social media.

Years ago, businesses promoted themselves through the use of newspaper ads, radio ads, and billboards. While those methods are still in use today, it's more about the clicks. How many people clicked on your social media ad, how many of them went to your website, and how long were they on your page? That's right. You can keep your company name in front of potential clients at very little expense.

Many social media sites, such as Facebook, LinkedIn, and X (formerly Twitter), are available today. It's all about branding and having a compelling, honest, and consistent message that resonates with your target market.

While social media is my favorite medium, many other ways exist to reach a large audience. You can start a blog or host a special event. You can sponsor charitable events to support local charities. These types of activities can elevate your image in your community. People will associate you and your business with community support, which can be a differentiator for you compared to your competition. This will humanize you and your company.

While branding your company, you must deliver exceptional service to your clients. It won't help to have your name out there if your customer satisfaction rating on Google is poor. When you provide products or services to clients, ask them to leave a Google review. The more reviews you can accumulate, the more credibility your business rating will have.

Outstanding service will lead to high satisfaction ratings. Disgruntled customers will leave a poor rating and a negative comment. Seventy-nine percent of unhappy customers will tell others about their experience, so when there is a complaint, make sure that you do everything possible to make it right, even if the customer was in error. Do it quickly so that the experience doesn't escalate. If it costs you a few dollars to achieve customer satisfaction, it will be money well spent. Negative Google reviews stay there for people to see and can damage your Google score. Why is the Google rating so important? Many people rely on those reviews when choosing who to do business with.

Periodic surveys with customers can help you uncover negative thoughts from customers. You may not even have realized that there was a problem. These surveys can be done on social media or through a program called SurveyMonkey.

Retaining an existing satisfied customer is cheaper and easier than attracting a new one. Building a list of customer emails can be very helpful. Some customers may be reluctant to provide one for fear of constantly being solicited, so you can incentivize them with a coupon offer if they provide you with their email. You can do the same if they like and follow you on social media. Be careful not to barrage them with emails. There are companies that send me multiple emails each day. I end up deleting the emails without opening them and often blocking their emails. Don't be that company. Once per week with special offers is more than enough. If you don't have a substantial number of email addresses accumulated, you can request that your local Chamber of Commerce send out an email blast for you. There is usually a small fee charged to members.

Posting weekly special offers or coupons on social media can keep clients engaged. Posting other interesting content like recipes or support for local events can also keep clients and others engaged and help you build a larger audience.

Be careful what you post. Once published online, those posts can be shared, reposted, and seen even if you delete them. Do not post any divisive or political content on your business social media sites, as there will always be those who will disagree or condemn you for your opinions. That is the sad truth of the cancel culture environment in which we live. Each social media site where you create a page is, in essence, a storefront for your business. Stick to business.

It is important to post regularly on your social media sites. Keep your audience engaged. In addition to posting about special offers, you can post about work anniversaries for your employees, new products and services you now have available, menus (if you are a restaurant), positive messages about community activities, and even free professional advice in your chosen field.

Chapter 12: Human Capital – Human Resource

One of the most valuable assets of a company is its employees. Yes, employees come and go to some extent. Turnover is part of owning and running a business. Successful companies nurture, reward, and value their employees and thus will have less turnover. When an employee is hired, there is generally an onboarding process. This process includes familiarizing them with company procedures but also involves investing time and effort to train the employee to perform their job duties. Time is money. The more turnover you have, the more money you spend on training. So, it would make sense to focus a reasonable amount of time and energy on training your staff well and showing them that they are appreciated. This, in turn, will reduce employee turnover and save you money on recruiting and training new employees.

You can begin by examining your current work environment. What kind of work environment exists in your workplace? Is it challenging? Is it a place where employees feel they can collaborate with other employees? Do the employees feel appreciated and supported? Are they well trained? Have you created a culture within your workplace where everyone works as a team to help the company reach its goals? Do your employees even know what the company's goals are? If they don't know the company goals, how will they know if they are being achieved?

How much information do you share about your company's goals with your employees? If you don't share this kind of information with them, how will they know if they are meeting your expectations or that of the company? Your employees must have benchmarks. They must understand your expectations and how they fit into the company's overall goals. If you are a manufacturer, how many parts must be manufactured daily? If you are a retail or sales organization, how many sales are required daily, weekly, monthly, or annually to meet your profitability goals?

Obviously, proprietary and financial information should not be shared with all of your employees, but there needs to be a metric to measure success. Then, your employees can buy into your goals and hopefully be motivated to help you achieve them. Make your employees feel they play a big part in the company's success. In doing so, they can take pride in their role in assisting the company to achieve it. This will give them a feeling of accomplishment and give their work more purpose.

Culture

We have been discussing your work environment. It should be one where employees are motivated and can work as a team to achieve goals. This is the culture you want to establish in your business. With that in mind, what characteristics will you look for when interviewing prospective employees? This will, of course, depend on your industry and the job description you are recruiting for. One of the most crucial characteristics is work ethic. Can they continue to work with distractions that may exist around them? Can they stay focused? Will they work until the job is done, or will they be watching the clock for the end of their shift? Can they work independently and in a team environment? Can they get along with and work well with others? Do they have the intelligence and skills to grow with your company and take on more responsibility when the opportunity arises?

I have always advocated hiring based on ability, intelligence, work ethic, and skill set. In my opinion, nothing else really matters. It's about building a team that collaborates well and elevates your business.

Where Do You Find These Candidates?

There are many methods available to recruit prospective employees. Sometimes, your best source is referrals from your current employees. Job fairs are another source. Many Chambers of Commerce sponsor such events. College campuses also have job fairs. There are several online recruiting sites, such as Indeed or Zip Recruiter. I have had very little success with those in the past. I have had success posting jobs on LinkedIn. Last but not least, you can engage a professional recruiter. The benefit of using an experienced recruiter is that they will look for the precise skillset you tell them you want. The downside is that you will pay the recruiter 10 to 20% of your candidate's annual salary. That means that the cost of hiring that employee to your company went from possibly $75,000 to $90,000 in the first year. It will likely be worth it if you find the employee who brings the skillset you are looking for.

The Interview

The goal of the interview should be to ascertain whether the employee fits your company's needs. Do they have all of the qualities we have discussed previously?

You can ask many questions, but you are not

allowed to ask certain ones, such as the candidate's age, medical conditions, marriage status, whether they have children, sexual preference, religion, etc.

I have found it more effective to ask open-ended questions like "Tell me about yourself?" After describing the job demands, "Are there any job duties that you would not be able to perform?" "Tell me about your last job." "What did you like and not like about the job?" Asking open-ended questions encourages the candidates to talk about themselves.

You are permitted to run background checks as long as you notify the candidate of your desire to do so. This is advisable if your candidate will handle money or have access to sensitive information. If your candidate lists references on their resume, you will likely waste your time contacting them as no one will provide a reference that would speak ill of them. Contacting prior employers can be a challenge as well. Employers are not likely to share much in the way of helpful information for fear of a slander suit. They may, however, confirm the employment and job duties.

Some companies also use personality profile tests to determine whether a candidate's personality suits the job description. This can sometimes be an effective tool.

Sometimes, it feels like your hands are tied when determining if a candidate would be a good hire for your company.

Onboarding-Orientation

When you have finally chosen a candidate to fill a position with your company, the next step is to go through the onboarding and training process. It is common for the new employee to be nervous but eager to get started. Be careful not to overwhelm them. The first day is crucial to ensuring the employee will show up on day two.

After the employee completes the paperwork, they are ready to go, but are you prepared to go? Is their workspace set up for them to work? You must be prepared and have a well-thought-out and effective onboarding and training process. This will set the tone for your new employee's success.

You should begin by familiarizing the new employee with their surroundings. Where is their work space? Where are the restrooms? Where should they park their vehicle? It seems simple enough, but the employer is often unprepared to welcome a new employee.

It is essential to introduce the new employee to the rest of the team so they know who to contact if they have questions. I believe that assigning a peer mentor is helpful. That individual should be one of your most experienced and trusted employees. Explain the hierarchy so the new employee knows who to report to.

So, let the training begin. Keep it simple. Start with easy tasks and build from there. The training process is a marathon, not a sprint. You should remember that everyone learns at a different pace and style. Some can read instructions and get it. Some are more visual and hands-on. Take time to determine the employee's learning style and adjust your training process appropriately. You have just made a substantial investment in this employee. You will want to see a return on your investment. The return on your investment is realized when this new hire becomes an effective employee.

Compensation

Your payroll will likely be your single most significant expense. There is no one-size-fits-all solution. Paying employees a fair wage is essential to retaining good employees, but who determines a fair salary?

If you are a union shop, it is simple. You negotiate the employees' wages with the union. Everyone starts at the same hourly wage, and all non-management employees receive the same wage, depending on their job description. Seems fair, right? But is it? How do you reward your most valuable employees? You can't? So, where is the motivation for an employee to work harder? Perhaps the hope for a promotion is the motivation.

So, what if you are not a union shop? How do you determine what is an appropriate wage? One way is to do research. You can find out what other businesses similar to yours are paying in your geographical area. Hourly wages can differ significantly from one geographical area to another. For example, in Ohio, if you were to google the hourly wage for a mechanic in the State of Ohio in 2024, it would be $24.10. In Mansfield, Ohio, the average hourly wage is $26.90. It can be very drastic from state to state. The cost of living will vary by geographical area, which will, in turn, cause the labor cost to vary.

It boils down to what the employee is worth to you and your business and what you can afford to pay. To attract quality employees, you may have to pay more than you want and pay them more than your existing employees earn. As distasteful as that seems, what is the alternative? Do you want to pass up an opportunity to add valuable talent to your staff? You can't necessarily afford to increase every existing employee's wage to match the new employee. I have always felt that it is divisive and unproductive for employees to share salary information with other employees, so I advise them not to. Of course, in the end, I can't legally prevent it.

Employers must review their employees' wage and benefit packages annually. Employees need to see growth in their salaries from year to year. Your cost of doing business goes up each year, and so does your employee's cost of living.

Benefits

A robust benefits package can help attract and retain employees while providing a living salary. Benefits such as medical coverage can be expensive and sometimes cost-prohibitive for many small businesses. Employers wishing to dip their toe in the water, so to speak, can begin with a plan that will at least provide the employees with minimum health benefits. Employers can also offer other medical options such as disability, vision, dental, and other benefits.

A retirement plan such as a 401k plan also appeals to prospective job applicants when looking for a new job. Offering a benefits package doesn't need to be done all at once. Each year, when you review your company's financial performance, you can add benefits when they are affordable. Adding something new to your benefits package each year improves employee morale. Employees will see your effort to provide for their financial needs and security.

Incentives and Bonuses

Another way to incentivize and reward your employees is to allow them to share in the company's success. Your company should show a profit if it reaches predetermined benchmarks or goals. The best way to ensure that you achieve those goals is to share those goals with your employees. Your goals can be tied to annual new sales, manufacturing output, or any benchmark appropriate to your industry. By doing this, your employees will have some skin in the game, so to speak. Your servers may be encouraged to upsell your patrons if you are a restaurant. Perhaps pushing to sell appetizers or desserts. If they achieve certain levels, then a bonus may be earned. If you are a sales organization, then there should be a sales production expectation in place. If they exceed that expectation, then they could earn additional compensation. Using incentives encourages employees to exceed expectations, which helps your business to exceed your company's expectations overall. Allowing your employees to share in your company's success is never bad.

Company Handbook

Every company, regardless of size, should have a company handbook. A well-written handbook spells out what is expected of your employees. What is the appropriate dress code for employees while on the job? This dress code may vary from one employee to another based on their job description. If they work in the warehouse or stock room, then a T-shirt and jeans may be fine, but if they are working with customers, then a business casual may be required. Is the dress code even enforceable if you don't have it written so they can read and understand it?

Your handbook can explain your benefits, such as vacation days, sick days, and holiday pay, and spell out procedures for requesting time off.

Your handbook can also spell out your expectations and rules and the consequences of not following them. A handbook can be your defense when there is a dispute between employer and employee.

Your handbook should be detailed, precise, and complete. It is essential that each employee receive one and that they sign a letter or form stating that they received it.

In this world of litigation, it is necessary to protect yourself.

Resources

Most small businesses don't have the money to hire a human resource professional. There are resources available to you. There are software companies that offer HR packages. The cost will vary by company size. Some have a minimum fee plus a per-employee charge. The cost is insignificant compared to the cost of hiring a professional. You can also hire HR firms.

Many payroll companies offer an HR platform as part of their package. The cost will again vary based on your number of employees and your chosen package.

I encourage you to research the options available to determine which best suits your needs and budget.

Discipline-Termination

Terminating an employee for disciplinary reasons can be painful and uncomfortable. Your handbook must clearly state for what reasons an employee can be terminated. When an employee violates conditions of employment, as spelled out in your handbook, some steps should be followed. First, you should approach the employee and discuss the violation so the employee understands how they violated the rules. Then, they should be directed to take corrective measures to avoid repeating the violation. If the violation is repeated, then a warning should be given to the employee as to what the consequences are for further abuses. Termination of employment is the next step should the employee continue to ignore the rules.

All conversations with the employee should be private and well-documented in the employee's file. This will ensure that you have documentation to support your termination decision should a wrongful termination lawsuit be filed against you or the employee file for unemployment.

When an employee has left you, you may receive a call from another business with which your former employee is seeking employment. Be careful what you share. I have made it a practice only to confirm the dates of employment and job description. In today's litigious environment, you need to protect yourself. Relaying any personal thoughts or opinions about the employee can cause you and your company harm.

Chapter 13: Managing Financials

One of the most essential tasks in owning or managing a business is monitoring its financial position. Your first step is establishing a budget that fits well within your projected revenue. There will be fixed expenses like rent, utilities, cost of goods, and such that are not flexible. There are other flexible expenses, such as marketing. You have to evaluate each expense to determine whether it is necessary and how that expense benefits your business. Will there be a return on that investment? Is there a more economical way of accomplishing the same thing and getting the same or a better result?

Monitoring results regularly will help you make necessary adjustments quickly and avoid deficit spending. The best way to monitor your financials is to run monthly financial reports. While these reports are only a snapshot, you can see how the company's financial position is trending by running them monthly. You can choose from several accounting software programs, and all of them should be able to track your spending trends and your company's profitability. PC Magazine names FreshBooks and QuickBooks as their top two choices for small businesses. These programs are purchased on a monthly subscription basis, and as of August 2024, the FreshBooks monthly cost ranged from $7.60 to $24.00 versus QuickBooks's $17.50 to $117.50. The more robust the program, the higher the price. The main thing is to ensure that whichever program level you choose will meet your current needs and have the features you will need as your business grows. You may want to consult your CPA before making the purchase.

One of the key functions of your accounting software is to provide you with financial reporting. It should be able to generate profit and loss (also known as an income statement) and balance sheet reports. These reports are crucial for understanding your business's financial health and should be run monthly in the early years of your business and at least quarterly once your company is well established.

Profit and Loss (Income Statement)

Your profit and loss statement is simply a snapshot of a specific period of time. It can provide you with financial data for a month, year-to-date, or for the entire year. The report begins by providing you with your income information and will break it down by source. The report will then show all of your expenses, including advertising and promotion, depreciation expenses, wages, and supplies and equipment. Every dollar spent and expense incurred will be revealed in this report.

Balance Sheet

Your company's balance sheet lists all of its assets, including bank account balances, real estate, equipment, and inventory. The report will provide the value line by line and then give a total of your assets. Your company's total liabilities will then be shown, including all debt and accounts payable. The difference between your total assets and liabilities will equal your net worth.

So, why is it so essential to run these reports frequently? Each report is, again, a snapshot in time. By looking at these reports, you can see trends. Is your income growing, stagnant, or shrinking? Are your expenses going up, and if so, in what category? Are the expenditures growing at a faster pace than the income? If your costs are increasing faster, what corrective measures can you implement to control the growth in the expenses?

Early in a business venture, it is not unusual for expenses to be higher than your income. Establishing a business takes time, and start-up costs are associated with it. That is why having a cash reserve before opening your doors is vital. You have advertising expenses to promote your business. You have supplies and equipment to buy.

You have employees to hire. You have rent. You have all these expenses before opening your business and before you can generate any income. You have to be prepared for that. Be patient, but monitor your progress regularly.

In the following two pages, you will find an Income Statement (Profit and loss) and a Balance Sheet illustration of the same small manufacturer shown in the Pro Forma at the end of year one.

Income Statement
For the Year Ending One

Income Statement		
Sales	500,000	100.00%
Cost of goods sold	275,000	55.00%
Depreciation	60,000	12.00%
Total cost of goods sold	335,000	67.00%
Gross Margin	165,000	33.00%
Other Costs		
Selling general and administrative	117,325	23.47%
Depreciation	4,300	0.86%
Interest expense term loan	20,655	4.13%
Interest expense line of credit	-	0.00%
Total other costs	142,280	28.46%
Net income before income tax	22,720	4.54%
Income tax	5,680	1.14%
Net Income	17,040	3.41%

Cash Flow for the Year Ending One	
Net income	17,040
Add depreciation	64,300
Deduct payment of principal long term debt	(81,250)
Deduct payment of principal line of credit	-
Change in accounts receivable	(83,333)
Change in inventory	(750)
Change in accounts payable	32,246
Cash flow	(51,747)
Borrow on line of credit	31,747
Decrease in cash	(20,000)

Balance Sheet
End of Year One

Assets	
Cash	5,000
Accounts receivable	83,333
Inventory	25,750
Total Current Assets	114,083
Property and equipment	450,000
Accumulated depreciation	(64,300)
Net book value	385,700
Total Assets	499,783
Liabilities and Equity	
Accounts payable	32,246
Line of credit payable	31,747
Current portion of long term debt	85,407
Total current liabilities	149,400
Long term debt	368,750
Less current maturities	85,407
Net long-term debt	283,343
Total liabilities	432,743
Equity	
Common Stock	50,000
Retained earnings beginning of year	-
Net income (Loss)	
Retained earnings end of year	17,040
Total Equity	67,040
Total liabilities and equity	499,783

Assumptions:
Sales $500,000
Gross Margin 33%
SG&A $117,325
Days in accounts receivable 60+
Days in accounts payable 30
Minimum cash balance 5,000.

Chapter 14: Protecting Your Investment

When opening a business, you need a professional team on your side. We already discussed the importance of having an attorney for legal advice and a CPA for financial advice. Another important member of your team should be an insurance agent. I recommend an agent who is well-versed in business insurance and represents an independent insurance agency. Independent agencies represent several insurance carriers, so they have more coverage and pricing options to offer.

Property Insurance

The property portion of the policy will cover your building, equipment, and inventory. Adding a replacement cost endorsement will prevent an insurance company from depreciating the value of the covered property. A deductible will be applied in the event of a loss. For example, if a wind storm were to damage your roof, a deductible would be paid by the insured business, perhaps $2,500, then the insurance company would pay the balance. If there were no replacement cost endorsement, then the roof would be depreciated based on its age. Your insurance agent would calculate the replacement cost value of your building, and that should be your coverage limit for the building. The replacement cost endorsement should also apply to your business personal property, including your equipment and inventory. Usually, the same deductible on the building would apply to your business' personal property.

If you take valuable equipment off your business premises to a job site, you would want to purchase inland marine coverage, as a standard policy limits coverage for property taken off premises.

Most insurance companies will base your coverage eligibility and premium on past claims experience. I advise you to carry a high deductible on your property coverage. A high deductible will lower the cost of your insurance, and it is not in your best interest to turn in small claims. Turning in multiple claims could result in a non-renewal from your company or an increase in your premium.

Liability

Liability coverage provides coverage if you cause injury or property damage to another party through regular business operations. Carrying a high limit of liability is advisable. In the current environment, the cost of settling a legal dispute may substantially exceed the actual value of the injury or damage caused.

Business Auto

When your business owns or operates a vehicle during normal business operations, you need a business auto policy, which may also be referred to as a commercial auto policy. The vehicle could be used to deliver, service customers, or haul goods to various locations. This coverage may be needed for a private passenger vehicle or a semi-tractor trailer. The coverage options will usually include liability, collision, and comprehensive coverage. You may also want to add optional coverage, such as uninsured motorists and roadside assistance. You should discuss all of the coverage options with your agent, as the coverage may differ from one state to another.

Workers Compensation

Workers' compensation is necessary regardless of the job description or duties. This coverage will protect you if your employees get injured while performing work associated with their jobs.

Make sure your agent understands all of your business activities so that you can prevent gaps in coverage.

Cyber Insurance Coverage

In today's digital world, hackers may risk your

intellectual property, client information, patents, and other proprietary information. The cost of diagnostics to determine whether you have been hacked will cost you many thousands of dollars. While every business should have robust security software to protect your data, that may not be enough.

Employment Practices

When an employee is disgruntled and feels wronged by the company, they may choose to file a discrimination or wrongful termination suit against you. These lawsuits are expensive to defend and can severely damage a company's reputation. This coverage is vital in protecting your business.

Directors and Officer Coverage

This coverage will protect company directors and officers from a lawsuit that may put their personal assets at risk. It may come into play when fiduciary decisions are made or breaches occur that financially put the company at risk. Stockholders may bring these suits or creditors of the company.

Business Income

Business income insurance will provide you with income if a fire or other catastrophic event prevents you from being able to use your facilities. This coverage will provide you with funds to keep your business afloat. You can use the money to continue to pay your employees so they don't seek employment elsewhere. This is an essential coverage. This coverage is based on your total annual revenue.

Chapter 15: SWOT

Periodically, it is crucial to review your competitive position in the marketplace. Are you over-priced? Are you underpriced? Are you delivering products and services efficiently and effectively? What are your strengths and weaknesses versus your competition?

SWOT is the acronym for Strengths - Weaknesses - Opportunities - Threats.

The business world constantly changes due to new products, technology, and the economic environment. Staying current and informed about these changes is vital to keeping your business viable and competitive.

I recommend that you perform this simple task at least every six months. List your company's strengths, weaknesses, opportunities, and threats. Can you take advantage of your strengths and maximize their benefits? What opportunities are you missing out on, and how can you adjust your business operations to take advantage of those opportunities? If there is a weakness, what can you do to turn that weakness into an area of strength? Will it take an additional investment in technology or staff training? Is there a severe threat that can cause your business to lose sales revenue?

I've included this short chapter to remind you to constantly be 'minding your business.' In my opinion, there is no holding steady. You are either moving forward or falling behind. A holding pattern is a losing strategy.

You want your business to be forward-looking. You want to always be on the lookout for opportunities, whether they involve a new product or service you can provide or an acquisition opportunity.

Always be aware of changes in your industry and be prepared to adjust. This can be the differentiator between you and your competition.

Chapter 16: Leadership

Whether you are a business owner or a manager, people will look to you for leadership. It is up to you to decide what kind of leader you want to be; not everyone inherently possesses the skill set to be a leader.

Can you provide the leadership to run a company? Let's examine some of the traits needed to be a good leader.

Intelligence:

Employees expect that the owner/manager has the intelligence to lead. A high IQ or a college degree does not automatically make you a leader. Leading people requires more. Do you possess emotional stability, self-awareness, and confidence to lead others?

Integrity:

Do you have a moral compass? Can you deal with people and situations honestly and thoughtfully? Employees need to know that they can trust you. They need to know what to expect from you. Not all situations are black and white. Can you see options beyond the cut-and-dry rules to resolve problems, or will your employees see you as a company bureaucrat with little concern for the employee's needs?

Energy:

Are you the leader who shows effort in engaging with your employees or one who remains in your office all day? That is not leadership. When managers work with their employees side-by-side and assist in getting things done, they show leadership. That trait goes a long way toward building trust and respect.

Communication:

Owners/managers must communicate openly and honestly with their employees, both orally and in writing. Employees must understand what management expects and that communication is consistent and clear. Ambiguous communications lead to confusion and misinterpretation, which in turn leads to unnecessary frustration on the part of the employees.

A leader is charged with being decisive when making decisions. Many leaders make decisions without input from employees, which is an autocratic leadership decision-making style. This style can lead to employee resentment, as sometimes these decisions don't consider how they will impact the employees and their ability to do their jobs.

Employees may feel that their opinions are respected and valued when participating in decision-making. This is a democratic decision-making style. There will be decisions where this style would not be appropriate. A company's inner workings and financials should not always be shared.

There are many management styles. Some support their employees, provide specific directions, and provide positive feedback. Others are participative leaders who include employees in important decisions.

Servant leaders prioritize their employees. Richard Branson stated, "Clients don't come first. Employees come first. If you care for your employees, they will care for your clients." This is the very essence of servant leadership. Servant leaders are well respected by their employees, and this leadership style creates a loyal staff.

A servant leader supports, encourages, and empowers their employees. A servant leader's qualities are apparent not just in the workplace but in the community as a whole. This is who they are.

Some leaders see employees as tools and provide little emotional support. They don't include them in decision-making or consider their feelings when changing business operations. These are abusive leaders. They can often treat employees rudely and foster discontent in the workplace. Sybil

Stershic stated, "The way your employees feel is the way your customers will feel."

How employees deal with the day-to-day responsibilities of their jobs may depend on their personality traits. Each employee is unique but might possess one of the following personality traits: openness, conscientiousness, extraversion, agreeableness, or neuroticism. A leader needs to identify those traits in their employees as some personalities may not fit some job descriptions well.

Putting employees in positions that don't suit their personalities could be disastrous. The textbook Principles of Management Version 4.0, published by FlatWorld, identifies these traits.

- Openness: This trait lends to being curious, original, intellectual, creative, and open to new ideas.

- Conscientiousness: This trait refers to someone who is organized, systematic, punctual, achievement-oriented, and dependable.

- Extraversion: This person is outgoing, talkative, and sociable.

- Agreeableness: The degree to which someone is affable, tolerant, trusting, and earnest.

- Neuroticism: This personality trait describes someone who is anxious, irritable, and temperamental.

Identifying these traits in your employees can help you, as a leader, place them in positions where they are most likely to be successful. For example, a stressful position demanding patience may not be a good position for someone with a neurotic trait. These traits may not be apparent at the time when you first interview a job candidate. Personality profile tests can sometimes help to identify these traits.

In the end, gaining the respect of your employees can be challenging for many reasons. The leader may not possess or have developed those skills yet, or some employees may naturally have little respect for authority figures. Putting your employees where they can succeed and feel valued will go a long way toward gaining their trust and respect. Consistently treating all of your employees with the same level of respect and consideration will also help.

Chapter 17: Managing Operations

The key to any business's continued success is managing day-to-day operations. You must constantly review efficiencies, time management, and operational processes. You can create more of everything except time, so it is vital that your company make the best use of the time you have.

This chapter will discuss some simple ways to improve efficiencies for you and your staff.

Time Management:

Have each department make a list of their daily activities. Then, review and prioritize the list based on the importance of each activity. Meet with each department to review the list. Are there unnecessary activities? Does another department duplicate some activities? Is there a more efficient way of processing those activities? Always look for time-saving tools or automation that can save time and money. Regular meetings with your teams can uncover opportunities not previously considered.

Emails:

If you are like me, you probably receive dozens of emails daily that you don't need to read. Set up a priority list of what emails you must deal with daily. Are you receiving emails that someone else in the company should be handling? Our company has separate email addresses for accounting, management, and individual departments and a general contact email box for customers, which our customer service representatives manage. Not every staff member needs to see every email that is sent to our company. You would be surprised how much time is saved daily by this simple adjustment in our operations. Using emails and DocuSign software also saves time and money and provides a more efficient way of communicating with clients and suppliers.

Meetings:

Prepare an agenda when meeting with staff or outside vendors. Without an agenda, a meeting can go on much longer than planned. Everyone gets off track discussing last night's game, their pet peeves, and whatever else pops into their minds. Stay focused and stick to the agenda.

Office Distractions:

Many employees will be social and want to discuss their family, their activities, or a new recipe they tried. Not only is the person sharing the information not working, but they are preventing others from performing their tasks. While you want there to be a sense of camaraderie among your team, you want to discourage prolonged conversations that are not work-related.

Sense of Urgency:

Perform tasks with a sense of urgency. Have a list of tasks to complete and focus on checking them off individually. Complete each one before moving on to the next. Revisiting the same task sometimes can't be avoided when you are waiting for a response or additional information, but in general, get the task done and move on. Try to instill that same mindset in your employees. You and your employees will feel a sense of achievement at the end of the day if everything on their lists is completed.

Phone Calls:

Throughout the day, you may receive dozens of calls. Many of these calls can be handled by other staff members or perhaps don't need to be taken at all. They can distract you from completing your daily activities. If you have a receptionist or secretary taking the calls, you may want to instruct that person to filter out the unnecessary calls and put them into your voicemail. At the end of the day, you can review the voicemails and determine which ones need a callback.

The Unexpected Visitor:

In many industries, vendors, and salespeople drop in unexpectedly for a visit. Remember that they are business people who are also trying to do their jobs. If you have a few minutes, greet them politely but encourage them to set up appointments in the future. It would be more productive for all concerned to have an appointment so that you can give them a reasonable amount of time to discuss the subject matter.

Schedules:

Make sure that your staff shares schedules. The Google Calendar can be considered a valuable tool. Your staff will know when you will have a meeting or when someone will be out of the office due to sickness, as well as your vacation information and lunch schedules. Make sure that everyone participates and keeps their calendar current.

Quality Control:

You should periodically audit your activities and those of your staff. You need to check for efficiency and accuracy. You also need to ensure that all company processes are being completed to the satisfaction of your clients and in a cost-effective way.

If you are manufacturing widgets, are those widgets done to the specifications your customers require? Is your staff producing the number per hour that meets your expectations? Are your salespeople performing at a level that provides value to your corporation? Are your customer service people handling the number of transactions that seem appropriate?

Reviewing these operational processes will help you keep in touch with your company's overall performance.

Chapter 18: Managing Your Clients

Good client management is essential to building relationships, improving customer experience, and growing your client base. Getting to know your clients and their needs is important to serve them in the future better. Understanding their needs enables you to anticipate their needs and address them as opportunities arise. If you are a car salesman and know your client has a large family, you can anticipate that your client may need a vehicle with a third row of seats to transport their family. When that vehicle becomes available at your dealership, that may create a sales opportunity.

Ask questions to your clients, gather information, including email addresses, and keep well-organized records. Software programs can assist you with keeping client information easily accessible.

Sometimes, you need to be a better listener than a salesperson. Ask probing, open-ended questions and let the prospect or client do the talking. Great salespeople are usually great listeners.

Once you have gathered information, document it. Don't assume that you will remember each transaction or communication. I'm sorry, but I think that no one is that good. By documenting transactions and communications, you are also protecting yourself. Clients often have short memories. At the time of purchase, you may have offered a feature or benefit that seemed unimportant to your client at the time. They need that benefit three months later and are upset they don't have it. Proper documentation can save you from an embarrassing situation or possibly a lawsuit.

An example may be a client who hires a landscaping company to design their garden. During the initial consultation, the landscaper suggests adding a smart irrigation system, but the client declines due to the extra cost. A few months later, during a heatwave, the client realizes their garden is suffering without the system and becomes frustrated when they remember the offer but can't locate the details. This is why you document everything, even if it seems insignificant at the time.

It is equally important that all of your employees are trained to document transactions and communications. There should be consistency throughout your organization in what information is gathered and documented. That should be part of your employee onboarding training.

So, you have done a good job of gathering client and prospect information, including emails. Now what? You can manage your emails through programs such as Constant Contact. This monthly subscription program costs from $12 to $80 per month. With this program, you can regularly communicate with prospects and clients for marketing, sales, and service purposes. Regularly keeping your name in front of your clients can improve customer retention and satisfaction.

Your client base may be your most important asset. Make sure that your clients know they can trust you to meet their needs. You should always exceed their expectations for quality products and services. Equally important is that they know that you value and appreciate their patronage and trust.

Chapter 19
Perpetuation Plan

No one likes to think about these things, but what will happen to your business if something unforeseen happens to you?

If you are a sole proprietor, does your family have the knowledge, training, and skills to keep the business going and growing, or will they be forced to sell? Will they know the company's value should they need to sell? Who will they sell your business to?

Your company's worth will change as your business grows. Keeping current with your financials, inventory, and other assets will make determining your company's actual net worth more accurate.

So, once again, who is going to buy the company? The first place to consider would be competitors. If it is a similar business, it can grow with the acquisition and eliminate a competitor simultaneously. They might find this an attractive opportunity.

Another option might be to sell the company internally to one or more employees. Those employees know the company well and may feel vested in seeing its success continue. They may also have an emotional attachment to the company. The question is, can they get the financing needed to complete the purchase? If they cannot get the funding, can the surviving spouse afford to take a chance that the company's success will continue, retain the debt themselves, and finance all or part of the sale?

If you have a partnership, LLC, or corporation with multiple owners, you will want to put plans in place to protect the business if one of the shareholders dies. The surviving partners may not want a partner's spouse, who may have no knowledge or skill to bring to the table, to come into the business in the event of their spouse's death. This can cause a great deal of disruption to the business operations.

The best way to prevent this scenario is to put a buy-sell agreement in place where the surviving partners can buy out the deceased partner's share in the business at a pre-determined price. Life insurance is often used to fund such an arrangement. The corporation purchases a life insurance policy for each member or partner equal to the value of their share in the business. The proceeds will then be paid to the surviving spouse, and the surviving members-partners become owners of the deceased member's shares. This is an excellent solution, as the surviving partners don't have to go into debt to buy the deceased member's share in the company.

How will the company replace the knowledge, talent, and skills lost when their partner died? The company could purchase additional life insurance to fund key man coverage. This life insurance would fund hiring someone with a similar skill set.

Retirement

What if the business owner is ready to retire? What is the plan for the company? Sell your share to your partners if you are in a partnership arrangement or have partners in an LLC or corporation.

Otherwise, the same options may exist. Sell to a competitor. Sell to your employees. If you have children in the agency, other options exist. A Family Trust may be an answer. With a trust, ownership of all your assets becomes part of the trust, and you and your spouse control the trust as trustees. Your children will become trustees when you and your spouse are deceased. You can continue to receive proceeds from the business through trust until both have passed; then, your children would have equal shares of your estate through the trust. The company can continue without interruption. This is just one option.

Consult your attorney.

Suggestion: If your children are your perpetuation plan, make them earn their way early in their employment with you. Let them start at the bottom and advance to leadership roles. Firstly, they will learn more about the workings of your company this way. Second, they will learn to appreciate how each position in the company fits into the overall company operation. Third, they will appreciate the accomplishment of reaching management positions within the company through hard work rather than having it handed to them. Fourth, your other employees will have more respect for them when they do reach leadership positions.

I have seen many situations where companies failed when the second or third generations took over because they felt entitled and didn't truly understand and appreciate the hard work it took to build the company and its reputation.

Lastly, if you sell to another entity, part of the agreement may require you to remain with the company for a transition period. This allows the new owners to acclimate to your operation and assists with retaining employees, suppliers, and clients.

Chapter 20:
It's a Wrap – Final Words of Wisdom

Being an entrepreneur can be rewarding and challenging. It certainly isn't for the faint of heart, and there are many ups and downs. Accomplishing your goals and becoming a successful business owner is a fantastic experience that should give you great pride.

Some people fear failure and are afraid to follow this path, but failure is not a life sentence; it's a life lesson. It is, indeed, the road less traveled.

When choosing this path, surround yourself with a good team: an attorney, CPA, insurance agent, and good employees who can not only help you grow but will grow with your company.

Be a servant leader who supports your employees and the community that supports you.

Protect the reputation of your company. Avoid controversial situations that could alienate potential clients. Even what you do as an individual can impact people's opinions of you and, in turn, affect your business.

Embrace new technologies and opportunities and keep current with market trends.

Be a "glass half full" type of person. Look for a

silver lining in every cloud. Try to turn a negative situation into an opportunity.

Stay humble. It is easy to get full of yourself when you are on top and victorious. Remember where you started, and never forget who helped you build your business. Keep the same characteristics and personality from when you started your business. To lose that is to lose the soul of your company.

Continue to monitor your financials and watch for trends that could threaten the financial stability of your company.

Be a winner in every situation. You either win, or you learn.

Try to buy locally when you can. Supporting local small businesses is always a good habit, even if it costs a little more. Remember, you are or were a small business.

Life is a team sport, and so is your business. Be a team player. Shine the light on others. Recognize and celebrate your employee's successes.

Be generous. Share your time and gifts with others.

No one is an island. Many people have influenced our lives and shared our journey. Be grateful for them; they helped us become who we are today.

Don't allow the business to take over your life. Your family needs you. Don't miss out on watching and participating in your children's growth. You can never get those years back. Your family should always come first.

One last bit of wisdom: never stop dreaming. Dream big and shoot for the stars. Never be satisfied. If you become satisfied, you may stagnate. There is no such thing as holding steady. Either you are moving forward or falling behind.

May you have a wonderful journey. I have.

www.ingramcontent.com/pod-product-compliance
Lightning Source LLC
Chambersburg PA
CBHW050443150626
46551CB00028B/1231

* 9 7 8 1 9 6 5 1 3 4 8 7 0 *